OUR BILL OF RIGHTS

AMERICAN FREEDOMS

A LOOK AT THE FIRST AMENDMENT

SARAH MACHAJEWSKI

PowerKiDS
press

NEW YORK

Published in 2019 by The Rosen Publishing Group, Inc.
29 East 21st Street, New York, NY 10010

Editor: Sharon Gleason
Book Design: Rachel Rising

Library of Congress Cataloging-in-Publication Data

Names: Machajewski, Sarah, author.
Title: American freedoms : a look at the First Amendment / Sarah Machajewski.
Description: New York : PowerKids Press, 2019. | Series: Our Bill of Rights | Includes index.
Identifiers: LCCN 2018015110| ISBN 9781538342909 (library bound) | ISBN 9781538342886 (pbk.) | ISBN 9781538342893 (6 pack)
Subjects: LCSH: Freedom of speech--United States--Juvenile literature. | United States. Constitution. 1st Amendment--Juvenile literature. | Freedom of religion--United States--Juvenile literature. | Freedom of the press--United States--Juvenile literature.
Classification: LCC KF4770 .M33 2018 | DDC 342.7308/53--dc23
LC record available at https://lccn.loc.gov/2018015110

CONTENTS

PROTECTING OUR BASIC FREEDOMS

What does it mean to have freedom? Centuries ago, this very question caused a revolution in the American colonies, and a new nation emerged as a result. When the first leaders of the new United States set out to create the laws of the land, they wove this question into the heart of many of the country's founding **documents**, including the U.S. Constitution.

Freedom was so important to Americans that they demanded it be protected by law. Today, nearly two and a half centuries later, these laws remain as important as ever. The First Amendment of the Constitution promises five basic freedoms to all U.S. citizens. Let's explore what they are, and why they're still so important.

THE BILL OF RIGHTS

When the authors of the Constitution presented the first copy at the Constitutional Convention, representatives from some states worried that it gave too much power to the central government. They refused to ratify, or approve, the Constitution until it contained more protection for individual freedoms. Ten changes, or amendments, were added to the Constitution in 1791. They're known as the Bill of Rights. They limit the government's power and protect citizens' basic freedoms.

The Bill of Rights is made of the first 10 amendments to the U.S. Constitution.

5

STEEPED IN HISTORY

The U.S. Constitution is steeped in history. It's nearly as old as the country itself. Hundreds of years ago, what's now the United States started as 13 British colonies. From Massachusetts in the North to Georgia in the South, the colonies were ruled by Great Britain and colonists were subjects of the king. Because of this relationship, colonists had to follow British rules and pay taxes to the crown, even though Britain was thousands of miles away.

In the 1760s, Britain tried to have more control over the colonists. The government forced colonists to pay taxes. Colonists were not happy with these taxes, especially because the colonies had no representation in British **Parliament**. By the 1770s, the call for change was growing strong.

KNOW YOUR RIGHTS!

Great Britain taxed the colonists on goods such as paper, tea, and stamps. The colonists also had to pay to cover the costs of keeping British soldiers in the colonies for protection after the French and Indian War, which lasted from 1754 to 1763.

Colonists made their desire for their rights known with protests such as the Boston Tea Party.

A REMARKABLE DOCUMENT

The American Revolution began in April 1775. At first, most colonists simply wanted the British government to listen to their grievances, or complaints. But as time passed, more colonists began to believe that the colonies should be independent. When the Continental Congress issued the Declaration of Independence on July 4, 1776, the United States was born.

The new United States was first governed by a set of laws called the Articles of Confederation. But in 1787, representatives from the states met in Philadelphia to make changes to the laws. They ended up writing a new document: the U.S. Constitution. This remarkable document identified the government's powers, established three branches of government, and set up a system of checks and balances.

Leaders in American government met in 1787 in Philadelphia, Pennsylvania, to change the Articles of Confederation. Instead, they made a new set of laws.

ARTICLES OF CONFEDERATION

The Articles of Confederation were the law of the United States from 1781 to 1789. The articles established a framework for how the new country's government should run. The Articles of Confederation allowed for a very weak central government. This made it hard for the government to enforce certain rules and policies. After a while, many government leaders felt the articles needed to be improved. A new constitution emerged as a result.

BACKGROUND TO THE BILL

The Constitution is a landmark document, but it isn't perfect. The original document states clearly what the U.S. government can do, but not what it can't do. Also, the Constitution doesn't talk much about individual rights and freedoms. In a country whose founders declared independence based on the idea of freedom, this was a glaring **omission**. Colonists could still remember what it was like to have their rights **violated** by a king with complete power and have no power to fight back.

Some representatives felt strongly that their state couldn't ratify, or approve, the Constitution unless these issues were addressed. They demanded that lawmakers add promises of individual liberties and freedoms. These promises became the first 10 amendments to the Constitution, which are known as the Bill of Rights.

Rhode Island was the final original state to ratify the Constitution. It did so in May 1790. The Bill of Rights officially became part of the Constitution in December 1791.

THE FATHER OF THE CONSTITUTION

JAMES MADISON

One of the Constitution's primary authors was James Madison, a Founding Father who later became secretary of state and fourth president of the United States. Madison was a representative of the state of Virginia, and he had helped write and pass its constitution. The Virginia Plan, written by Madison, was the basis for the U.S. Constitution. Madison also wrote 19 amendments in response to representatives' demands, and 10 were adopted as the Bill of Rights.

STARTING OFF STRONG

The Bill of Rights begins with a powerful First Amendment. It states: "Congress shall make no law respecting an establishment of religion, or **prohibiting** the free exercise thereof; or **abridging** the freedom of speech or of the press; or the right of the people peaceably to assemble, and to **petition** the Government for a **redress** of grievances."

This amendment addresses key freedoms. Americans were used to having certain freedoms, including the same rights as British citizens when they were under British rule. All the freedoms contained in the First Amendment existed at the time it was written. The amendment was intended to preserve the freedoms as they were. This amendment was written with the future in mind.

KNOW YOUR RIGHTS!

Some of the ideas contained in the U.S. Constitution were inspired by a British document called the Magna Carta, which promised individual rights, representative government, and more.

American colonists protested many of the British government's actions. Madison, in part, wrote the First Amendment to protect the right to protest. This engraving shows colonists protesting the British Stamp Act by burning papers in Boston in August 1764.

SEPARATION OF CHURCH AND STATE

Reread the first part of the First Amendment: "Congress shall make no law respecting an establishment of religion, or prohibiting the free exercise thereof." Put simply, it means that the government can't get involved in religion. This is commonly called "separation of church and state."

The first part of the phrase means that Congress can't establish a national religion. Historically, other countries have had national religions, but that can't happen in the United States. The second part of the phrase says the government can't keep citizens from practicing their religion—any religion. Remember that many people came to America to escape religious persecution, or bad treatment, in their home country. America was seen as a place of religious freedom, and the First Amendment protects that.

KNOW YOUR RIGHTS!

At the time of the Bill of Rights, some states (such as Massachusetts) had established state churches. The First Amendment protected those relationships and kept the federal government from changing them.

The United States is a place where people are free to practice any religion. It's important that people are free to believe what they want—and even more important to respect their beliefs, even if they're different than yours.

15

SPEAKING YOUR MIND

Imagine you have an idea, but saying it out loud would get you in trouble with the government. There are places around the world where this is a part of life. However, in the United States, the right to speak your mind is protected by law.

The First Amendment says Congress can't make any law that takes away citizens' freedom of speech or expression. This is based in the belief that a free and open exchange of ideas makes for a better society. For example, the freedom to say what you think may encourage tolerance and respect for other people's views. It's also a way for citizens to keep their government in check. People can publicly disagree with their government's actions without fear of punishment from that government.

KNOW YOUR RIGHTS!

The First Amendment protects all freedom of speech—even if it's offensive or **controversial**. Organizations such as the American Civil Liberties Union (ACLU) have defended hate speech in court on the basis that all speech must be protected.

Protests are freedom of speech in action. These people are practicing their right to free speech.

REASONABLE LIBERTY

The First Amendment may allow freedom of expression, but it's not **absolute**. Many people may think that they can say whatever they want, whenever they want, and cite the First Amendment as their reason why. However, there are some limitations. The First Amendment also doesn't protect people from the other consequences of their speech.

U.S. courts have spent centuries trying to determine what is and what isn't protected speech. Your right to not salute the American flag is protected. So is your right to protest war, use some offensive words, advertise products, and protest through symbolic actions. Speech judged to cause actions that harm others or to be **obscene** may not be protected by the First Amendment.

While freedom of speech is a powerful principle, it's important to remember there are limitations to it. In *Schenck v. United States*, Justice Oliver Wendell Holmes famously explained the limitation by using the example that people don't have the right to falsely shout "fire" in a crowded theater, because it puts others in harm's way.

SCHENCK V. UNITED STATES

In 1919, the U.S. Supreme Court heard a case that helped to set the limits of free speech. A man named Charles Schenck was arrested for handing out antiwar and antidraft leaflets during World War I. The government said he broke a law meant to prevent people from harming the war effort. Schenck argued that this law prevented citizens from speaking out against the war, violating their First Amendment right. The court ruled against Schenck, stating that the circumstances of war allowed freedom of speech to be limited.

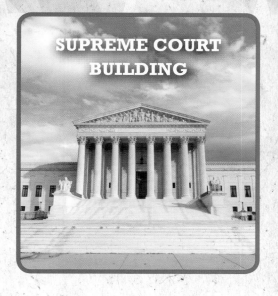

SUPREME COURT BUILDING

COMBATING CENSORSHIP

Freedom of the press is another important idea addressed in the First Amendment. It shares much of the same thinking that governs freedom of speech and expression, but it specifically relates to the press, or media.

Most historians agree that the root of this idea can be traced to the 1735 trial of John Peter Zenger. Zenger printed the *New-York Weekly Journal* newspaper, which published unfavorable opinions about New York's colonial governor, William Cosby. To silence the paper, Cosby had Zenger charged with libel. Libel is a false published statement against someone's character. Cosby also tried to use his power to **censor** the paper in other ways.

Ultimately, Zenger was found not guilty because the statements in question were true. This idea had such an impact that it later influenced the First Amendment.

KNOW YOUR RIGHTS!

Andrew Hamilton served as Zenger's lawyer, famously stating in trial: "The question before [you] is not of small or private concern. It is not the cause of one poor printer. . . . It is the best cause. It is the cause of liberty."

Events such as Zenger's trial demonstrated the need for protection of American liberties.

A FREE AND OPEN PRESS

At the time of the Constitution's writing, "the press" mostly meant newspapers. However, centuries later, the meaning of "the press" has grown. In recent decades, news outlets have grown to include newspapers, magazines, journals, radio programs, news programs on television and online, and a seemingly endless supply of Internet news sources. Many types of mass media exist in the United States, which is why ensuring their freedom is so important.

Under the First Amendment, the government can't **interfere** with what the media reports on or publishes. The media may report on the government's activities, reveal truths, and expose untruths without fear of censorship. A free and open press is a fundamental part of a free society. Without it, citizens couldn't be informed and aware.

KNOW YOUR RIGHTS!

Like freedom of speech, freedom of the press is not absolute. For example, copyright laws make it illegal to copy someone else's work.

Along with freedom comes responsibility. A free press is responsible for providing information that is fair and true.

ABOUT PEACEFUL ASSEMBLY

The next part of the First Amendment ensures "the right of the people to peaceably assemble." "Assemble" means to gather in groups. This part of the law means that people can freely gather as long as they are peaceful. Under law, the government doesn't have the right to stop them from gathering.

Remember again the time in which leaders created this law. In the past, it could be dangerous for people to gather to discuss their political beliefs. In Great Britain, laws prevented more than 50 people from gathering at one time without permission. This was, in part, to keep unfavorable opinions about the government from spreading. The framers of the Constitution valued the power of groups. In a free society, assembling in groups is a powerful tool that people can use to express their ideas.

The First Amendment protects all groups' right to gather, even if it's a group of people with unpopular or controversial ideas.

MODERN PROTESTS

Americans have exercised their right to peaceful protest throughout history. In the early 20th century, women fought for the right to vote by marching and holding rallies and meetings. In the 1960s, the civil rights movement included many peaceful protests, including the march on Washington where Dr. Martin Luther King Jr. made his famous "I Have a Dream" speech. Today, citizens are exercising their First Amendment rights by holding marches in favor of women's rights, stricter gun laws, and more.

MAKING YOUR VOICE HEARD

The last part of the First Amendment states that citizens have the right "to petition the Government for a redress of grievances." "To petition" means to bring a request to an authority. "Redress of grievances" means to correct a problem or issue. In other words, citizens can tell the government about things they don't like and ask the government to fix them.

This is an important part of the First Amendment, because it allows citizens to take action. Colonists once used petitions to change things, and people today sometimes do so as well. They write letters, make phone calls to representatives, protest, **lobby**, and gather signatures, which means that people write down their names to support an idea. No matter the method, petitioning is important because it raises awareness about important issues.

CHALLENGES TO THE FIRST AMENDMENT

The First Amendment has protected and promised freedoms since leaders added the Bill of Rights to the U.S. Constitution. However, that doesn't mean it has gone unchallenged. The U.S. Constitution has what's called an "elastic clause," which provides room for how its rules can be understood and applied. It is the task of the country's court systems to interpret the First Amendment when it comes under question in court.

One famous court case involving the First Amendment took place in 1969, when three students were suspended from school for wearing armbands to protest the Vietnam War. The school banned armbands, and the students wore them anyway. When the school suspended them, they sued. In the court case *Tinker v. Des Moines Independent School District*, the Supreme Court ruled in favor of the students, arguing that the armbands were not causing trouble, even though they made some people uncomfortable.

"It can hardly be argued that either students or teachers shed their constitutional rights to freedom of speech or expression at the schoolhouse gate," the Supreme Court famously stated in *Tinker v. Des Moines Independent School District.*

IMPORTANT AS EVER

This court case was not the first to challenge an issue using the First Amendment, nor was it the last. Citizens have brought many issues before the court, including the content of speeches, newspapers, books, and more. It's clear: people are willing to stand up for their rights. Given how valued the rights in the First Amendment are, people are willing to fight back when they feel others are challenging them.

It's important for all citizens to know and exercise their rights. Putting the First Amendment into practice will help keep American society free and open to new ideas, tolerant of others' beliefs, and willing to stand up to government actions. The First Amendment was written nearly 300 years ago, but it remains as important as ever.

GLOSSARY

abridge: To lessen the strength or effect of something.

absolute: Not subject to any limitation.

censor: To suppress parts of something.

controversial: Likely to give rise to disagreement.

document: A formal piece of writing.

interfere: To get in the way of something.

lobby: To seek to influence politicians or political groups.

obscene: Very offensive in a shocking way.

omission: Something that is left out.

parliament: A name for some lawmaking bodies.

petition: To make a request.

prohibit: To prevent from doing something.

redress: The act of righting a wrong.

violate: To fail to respect someone's rights.

INDEX

WEBSITES

Due to the changing nature of Internet links, PowerKids Press has developed an online list of websites related to the subject of this book. This site is updated regularly. Please use this link to access the list: www.powerkidslinks.com/obor/first